FAVORITE ALL TIME™ RECIPES $3.50

❧ GREY ❧ POUPON®

SIMPLY DELICIOUS RECIPES

D1515079

Discover more of your favorite recipes!

For additional titles write to:
Favorite All Time Recipes
7373 N. Cicero Ave.
Lincolnwood, IL 60646

ISBN: 0-7853-1571-3

Photography: Photo/Kevin Smith, Chicago
Photographers: Kevin Smith, Doug Hunter
Assistants: Jerry Cox, Greg Shapps
Food Stylists: Dianne Hugh, Tobe Lemoine, Teri Rys-Maki
Assistant Food Stylist: Kim Hartman
Photo Stylist: Diane Gurolnick

Pictured on the front cover: Sweet & Sour Mustard Pork *(page 72).*

Pictured on the back cover *(clockwise from top left):* Ham and Gouda Quesadilla Snacks *(page 4),* Mixed Salad with Raspberry Honey Dijon Dressing *(page 26)* and Smoked Turkey and Provolone Croissant *(page 48).*

♔ GREY ♔ POUPON®

SIMPLY DELICIOUS RECIPES

♛ GREY ♛ POUPON.

ONE OF LIFE'S SIMPLER PLEASURES

*F*rom sandwiches to gourmet main courses, hot dogs to steak, any dish can be enhanced with the zesty flavor of Grey Poupon® Mustard. These simple recipes will turn your everyday meals into extraordinary ones.

Did you know that Grey Poupon is naturally fat free and is a cholesterol-free food? Serving for serving, mayonnaise has **20 times** the amount of calories and **11 times** the amount of fat as Grey Poupon Dijon Mustard. A serving of mayonnaise has 100 calories and 11 grams of fat, while Grey Poupon Dijon Mustard has 5 calories and no fat. If cholesterol is a concern, mayonnaise has approximately 8 mg per serving, while Grey Poupon Dijon Mustard has *none*. So, whether you are using the recipes in this book or just adding a touch of flavor to a sandwich, keep in mind that using mustard instead of mayonnaise is a quick way to save on calories and fat without losing flavor.

The recipes in this book are easy to prepare and taste just glorious. Try Bistro Burgundy Stew (page 74); it uses classic

Grey Poupon Dijon—a velvety textured mustard, made with a special blend of mustard seeds, spices and white wine. For a bolder taste, use Grey Poupon Country Dijon; this hearty textured mustard is featured in Grilled Chicken Caesar Salad (page 32). Try using Grey Poupon Spicy Brown Mustard to liven up a sandwich. Or, for a new taste sensation, sample the Grey Poupon Specialty Mustards—Honey, Horseradish or Peppercorn. For easy-to-use convenience, there's original Grey Poupon Dijon in the squeeze bottle.

Whichever Grey Poupon mustard you choose, we are sure you'll find the taste to be "One of Life's Finer Pleasures."

APPETIZERS

HAM AND GOUDA QUESADILLA SNACKS

Makes 24 appetizers

1½ cups shredded smoked
   Gouda cheese
   (6 ounces)
1 cup chopped ham
   (4 ounces)
½ cup pitted ripe olives,
   chopped
¼ cup minced red onion

½ cup GREY POUPON
   COUNTRY DIJON
   Mustard
8 (6- or 7-inch) flour tortillas
Sour cream, chopped
   peppers, sliced pitted
   ripe olives and cilantro,
   for garnish

In small bowl, combine cheese, ham, olives and onion. Spread 1 tablespoon mustard on each tortilla; spread about ⅓ cup cheese mixture over half of each tortilla. Fold tortilla in half to cover filling.

In large nonstick skillet, over medium heat, heat filled tortillas for 4 minutes or until cheese melts, turning once. Cut each quesadilla into 3 wedges. Place on serving platter; garnish with sour cream, peppers, olives and cilantro.

Ham and Gouda Quesadilla Snacks

MOZZARELLA & TOMATO WITH LEMON DIJON DRESSING

Makes 6 appetizer servings

⅓ cup olive oil
¼ cup GREY POUPON COUNTRY DIJON Mustard*
2 tablespoons lemon juice
2 teaspoons finely chopped fresh basil leaves
½ teaspoon sugar

3 medium tomatoes, sliced
6 ounces mozzarella cheese, sliced
2 cups mixed salad greens
¼ cup coarsely chopped pitted ripe olives
Chopped fresh basil leaves

In small bowl, whisk oil, mustard, lemon juice, basil and sugar; set aside.

Arrange tomato and cheese slices over salad greens on serving platter. Top wit chopped olives and basil leaves; garnish as desired. Drizzle with prepared dressing before serving.

*Grey Poupon Peppercorn Mustard may be substituted for Country Dijon Mustard

ORANGE DIJON CHICKEN WINGS

Makes 24 appetizers

½ cup GREY POUPON COUNTRY DIJON Mustard
½ cup ketchup
⅓ cup orange marmalade
1 tablespoon reduced sodium soy sauce

1 tablespoon dried minced onion
1 clove garlic, crushed
12 chicken wings, split and tips removed

In small bowl, blend mustard, ketchup, marmalade, soy sauce, onion and garli Place chicken wings in plastic bag; coat with ½ cup mustard mixture. Refrigerate chicken wings and remaining mustard mixture for at least 1 hour.

Place chicken wings on baking sheet. Bake at 375°F for 20 minutes, pouring o any excess fat. Bake 20 to 25 minutes more or until done. Heat remaining mustard mixture until warm; serve as a dipping sauce with hot wings.

TIP: *Sauce may be used for basting chicken parts or ribs while grilling.*

Mozarella & Tomato wi
Lemon Dijon Dressi

BRUSCHETTA DIJON

Makes 18 appetizers

¼ cup olive oil, divided
1 clove garlic, minced
18 (¼-inch-thick) slices
   French bread
1½ cups chopped eggplant
½ cup chopped onion
½ cup diced red, yellow or
   green bell pepper
1 cup chopped tomato
¼ cup GREY POUPON
   COUNTRY DIJON
   Mustard

1 teaspoon dried oregano
   leaves
¼ cup chopped pitted ripe
   olives
2 tablespoons grated
   Parmesan cheese
Chopped parsley, for
   garnish

Combine 2 tablespoons oil and garlic. Arrange bread slices on baking sheets; brush tops with oil mixture. Set aside.

In large skillet, over medium heat, sauté eggplant, onion and bell pepper in remaining oil until tender. Stir in tomato; cook for 2 minutes. Add mustard, oregano and olives; heat through.

Broil bread slices for 1 minute or until golden. Top each toasted bread slice with about 1 tablespoon vegetable mixture. Sprinkle with Parmesan cheese; garnish with parsley. Serve warm.

Bruschetta Dij

LAYERED AVOCADO AND BLACK BEAN DIP

Makes 6 to 8 appetizer servings

2 ripe medium avocados, pitted and peeled
¼ cup GREY POUPON Dijon Mustard
2 tablespoons lime juice
¼ cup minced red onion
1 clove garlic, crushed
1 teaspoon chopped cilantro
1 to 2 teaspoons liquid hot pepper seasoning

1 (16-ounce) can black beans, rinsed and drained
½ cup dairy sour cream*
½ cup chopped tomato
Shredded Cheddar cheese, sliced pitted ripe olives and additional sour cream, for garnish
Tortilla chips

In electric blender container, combine avocados, mustard and lime juice until blended. Stir in onion, garlic, cilantro and hot pepper seasoning; set aside.

In medium bowl, mash black beans; combine with ½ cup sour cream. Spread black bean mixture on serving dish. Spread avocado mixture over bean layer. Top with tomato, cheese and olives. Garnish with additional sour cream. Serve with tortilla chips.

Lowfat sour cream may be substituted for regular sour cream.

SAVORY STUFFED MUSHROOMS

Makes 24 appetizers

24 large mushrooms
½ cup chopped green onions
1 tablespoon margarine or butter
½ teaspoon dried rosemary leaves
¼ cup dry white wine
¼ cup GREY POUPON COUNTRY DIJON Mustard

¾ cup plain dry bread crumbs
¾ cup shredded Swiss cheese (3 ounces)
1 egg, beaten
4 slices bacon, cooked and crumbled
Chopped parsley and grated Parmesan cheese, for garnish

Remove stems from mushrooms; reserve caps. Coarsely chop mushroom stems. In large skillet, over medium-high heat, sauté chopped stems and green onions in margarine or butter until tender. Stir in rosemary, wine and mustard; heat to a boil. Reduce heat to low; simmer for 3 minutes. Remove from heat; let stand 5 minutes. Stir in bread crumbs, cheese, egg and bacon. Spoon stuffing mixture into mushroom caps; place on baking sheet. Bake at 350°F for 12 to 15 minutes or until heated through. Garnish with parsley and cheese. Serve hot.

HOT CRABMEAT DIJON DIP

Makes 2 cups

8 ounces cream cheese,*
   softened
6 tablespoons GREY
   POUPON Dijon
   Mustard, divided**
¼ cup chili sauce
2 teaspoons prepared
   horseradish**
1 teaspoon lemon juice
1½ teaspoons chopped fresh
   dill, divided

1 (6-ounce) can crabmeat,
   drained and flaked
⅓ cup plain dry bread
   crumbs
1 tablespoon margarine or
   butter, melted
Vegetable crudités or
   assorted crackers, for
   dipping

In medium bowl, with electric mixer at medium speed, blend cream cheese, 5 tablespoons mustard, chili sauce, horseradish, lemon juice and 1 teaspoon dill. Stir in crabmeat. Spoon mixture into greased 1-quart shallow baking dish. Combine bread crumbs, margarine or butter and remaining mustard and dill; sprinkle over crab mixture. Bake at 350°F for 20 to 25 minutes or until heated through. Serve with vegetable crudités or assorted crackers.

Lowfat cream cheese may be substituted for regular cream cheese.

**6 tablespoons Grey Poupon Horseradish Mustard may be substituted for Dijon mustard; omit horseradish.*

BEEFY TORTILLA ROLLS

Makes 20 appetizers

¼ cup GREY POUPON
    COUNTRY DIJON
    Mustard
3 ounces cream cheese,
    softened
2 teaspoons prepared
    horseradish
2 teaspoons chopped
    cilantro or parsley

2 (10-inch) flour tortillas
1 cup torn spinach leaves
6 ounces thinly sliced deli
    roast beef
1 large tomato, cut into 8
    slices
    Lettuce leaves

In small bowl, combine mustard, cream cheese, horseradish and cilantro or parsley. Spread each flour tortilla with half the mustard mixture. Top each with half the spinach leaves, roast beef and tomato slices. Roll up each tortilla jelly-roll fashion. Wrap each roll in plastic wrap and chill at least 1 hour.*

To serve, cut each roll into 10 slices; arrange on lettuce-lined platter.

*Tortilla rolls may be frozen. To serve, thaw at room temperature for 1 hour before slicing.

HERBED STUFFED EGGS

Makes 24 appetizers

12 hard-cooked eggs
½ cup garlic and herb cheese
    spread
¼ cup mayonnaise*
¼ cup GREY POUPON
    Dijon Mustard

¼ cup finely chopped green
    onions
2 tablespoons finely chopped
    pimientos

Halve eggs lengthwise. Scoop out yolks into bowl; set egg white halves aside. Mash yolks; blend in cheese spread, mayonnaise, mustard, green onions and pimientos. Spoon or pipe yolk mixture into egg white halves. Chill until serving time.

*Lowfat mayonnaise may be substituted for regular mayonnaise.

Beefy Tortilla Rolls

SOUTH–OF–THE–BORDER QUICHE SQUARES

Makes 24 appetizers

1 (8-ounce) package refrigerated crescent dinner roll dough	1 cup milk
1½ cups shredded Monterey Jack and Colby cheese blend (6 ounces)	⅓ cup **GREY POUPON COUNTRY DIJON Mustard**
½ cup Ortega® Diced Green Chiles	1 tablespoon chopped cilantro or parsley
½ cup chopped onion	½ teaspoon chili powder
4 eggs, beaten	Chopped tomato and yellow and green bell peppers, for garnish

Unroll dough and press perforations together. Press dough on bottom and 1 inch up sides of greased 13×9×2-inch baking pan. Bake crust at 375°F for 5 to 8 minutes or until lightly golden. Remove from oven; sprinkle with half the cheese. Top with chiles, onion and remaining cheese.

In medium bowl, blend eggs, milk, mustard, cilantro or parsley and chili powder. Pour mixture evenly over cheese layer. Bake at 375°F for 25 to 30 minutes or until set. Cool 5 minutes. Garnish with tomato and bell peppers; cut into 2-inch squares. Serve hot.

South-of-the-Border
Quiche Square

HONEY DIJON BARBECUE RIBETTES

Makes 8 servings

2½ pounds baby back pork
   spareribs, split
2 cloves garlic, minced
1 tablespoon vegetable oil
⅔ cup chili sauce
⅓ cup GREY POUPON
   Dijon Mustard

¼ cup honey
6 thin lemon slices
½ teaspoon liquid hot pepper
   seasoning

Place ribs in large heavy pot; fill pot with water to cover ribs. Over high heat, heat to a boil; reduce heat. Cover; simmer for 30 to 40 minutes or until ribs are tender. Drain.

Meanwhile, in medium saucepan, over low heat, cook garlic in oil until tender. Stir in chili sauce, mustard, honey, lemon slices and hot pepper seasoning. Cook over medium heat until heated through, about 2 to 3 minutes. Brush ribs with prepared sauce. Grill over medium heat for 15 to 20 minutes or until done turning and brushing often with remaining sauce. Slice into individual pieces to serve; garnish as desired. Serve hot.

SMOKEY GREY POUPON BRIDGE MIX

Makes about 3 cups

1 (12-ounce) can Planters®
   Unsalted Mixed Nuts
⅓ cup GREY POUPON
   Dijon Mustard
2 tablespoons margarine or
   butter, melted

¾ teaspoon Wright's® Natural
   Hickory Seasoning
½ teaspoon garlic powder
1 cup sesame sticks

Place mixed nuts in shallow baking pan. Bake at 300°F for 20 minutes, stirring occasionally.

In medium bowl, blend mustard, margarine or butter, hickory seasoning and garlic powder. Stir in hot nuts until coated. Return coated nuts to baking pan. Bake at 300°F for 20 to 25 minutes or until nuts are browned and slightly dry. Stir in sesame sticks; cool. Store in airtight container.

Honey Dijon Barbecue
Ribbettes

SWEET & SOUR COCKTAIL MEATBALLS

Makes 32 appetizers

1 pound ground turkey
¾ cup plain dry bread
   crumbs
½ cup GREY POUPON
   Dijon Mustard, divided
½ cup chopped green onions,
   divided
1 egg, beaten
½ teaspoon ground ginger

½ teaspoon ground black
   pepper
1 (8-ounce) can pineapple
   chunks, undrained
⅓ cup firmly packed light
   brown sugar
¼ cup apple cider vinegar
¼ cup diced red bell pepper
1 teaspoon cornstarch

In large bowl, combine turkey, bread crumbs, ¼ cup mustard, ¼ cup green onions, egg, ginger and black pepper. Shape into 32 (1-inch) balls. Place in greased 13×9×2-inch baking pan. Bake at 350°F for 20 minutes.

Meanwhile, in medium saucepan, combine pineapple chunks with juice, sugar, vinegar, red bell pepper, cornstarch and remaining mustard and green onions. Cook over medium heat until sauce thickens and begins to boil. Spoon pineapple sauce over meatballs. Bake 5 to 7 minutes more or until meatballs are done. Spoon into serving dish and serve with toothpicks.

ZESTY SPINACH DIP

Makes 2 cups

1 cup dairy sour cream*
¼ cup GREY POUPON
   Dijon Mustard
1 (0.7-ounce) package
   Italian salad dressing
   mix
1 (10-ounce) package frozen
   chopped spinach,
   thawed and well drained

¼ cup finely grated carrot
2 tablespoons finely chopped
   red bell pepper
Hollowed green or red bell
   pepper cup, optional
Assorted vegetable
   crudités and crackers,
   for dipping

In medium bowl, blend sour cream, mustard and salad dressing mix. Stir in spinach, carrot and chopped bell pepper. Chill until serving time.

If desired, spoon dip into green or red bell pepper cup. Serve with crudités and crackers.

Lowfat sour cream may be substituted for regular sour cream.

SUNDRIED TOMATO CHEESE BALL

Makes 1-pound cheese ball

8 ounces cream cheese,*
   softened
1 cup shredded Cheddar
   cheese (4 ounces)
⅓ cup GREY POUPON
   COUNTRY DIJON
   Mustard
1 teaspoon dried basil leaves
1 clove garlic, crushed

½ teaspoon onion powder
¼ cup sundried tomatoes,**
   finely chopped
⅓ cup walnuts or pine nuts,
   toasted and chopped
Assorted crackers,
   breadsticks and bagel
   chips

In large bowl, with electric mixer at medium speed, mix cheeses, mustard, basil, garlic and onion powder until blended but not smooth. Stir in sundried tomatoes. Shape cheese mixture into a 5-inch ball; wrap and chill 1 hour. Roll cheese ball in chopped nuts. Wrap and chill until serving time.

Serve as a spread with assorted crackers, breadsticks and bagel chips.

*Lowfat cream cheese may be substituted for regular cream cheese.

**If sundried tomatoes are very dry, soften in warm water for 15 minutes. Drain before using.

PESTO BRIE

Makes 6 to 8 appetizer servings

2 tablespoons GREY
    POUPON Dijon
    Mustard
2 tablespoons prepared pesto
    sauce
1 (8-ounce) wheel Brie
    cheese

2 tablespoons Planters®
    Walnuts, finely chopped
Chopped tomatoes and
    fresh basil leaves, for
    garnish
Assorted crackers or
    breadsticks

In small bowl, blend mustard and pesto; set aside. Cut cheese in half horizontally. Place bottom half on greased baking sheet, cut-side up; spread with half the pesto mixture. Replace top of Brie, cut-side down; spread with remaining pesto mixture and sprinkle with nuts.

Bake at 350°F for 3 to 4 minutes or until cheese is slightly softened. *Do not overbake*. Transfer to serving dish. Garnish with chopped tomatoes and basil leaves. Serve with assorted crackers or breadsticks.

ANTIPASTO PLATTER

Makes 4 servings

¼ cup GREY POUPON
    Dijon Mustard
¼ cup dairy sour cream*
¼ cup buttermilk
¼ cup grated Parmesan
    cheese
1 teaspoon coarsely ground
    black pepper
½ head leaf lettuce, separated
    into leaves

2 ounces radicchio leaves
1 bunch endive, separated
    into leaves
8 ounces deli sliced ham
4 ounces deli sliced Swiss
    cheese
2 ounces deli sliced salami
1 medium tomato, cut into
    wedges
¼ cup whole ripe olives

In small bowl, whisk mustard, sour cream, buttermilk, Parmesan cheese and pepper until blended. Chill dressing until serving time.

Place lettuce, radicchio and endive on large serving platter; top with ham, Swiss cheese, salami, tomato and olives. Serve with prepared dressing.

*Lowfat sour cream may be substituted for regular sour cream.

Pesto Brie

SAVORY SAUSAGE MUSHROOM TURNOVERS

Makes 32 appetizers

1 (12-ounce) package frozen
  bulk pork sausage,
  thawed
1 cup chopped mushrooms
⅓ cup chopped onion
½ cup shredded Swiss cheese
  (2 ounces)
⅓ cup GREY POUPON
  COUNTRY DIJON
  Mustard

2 tablespoons diced red bell
  pepper
½ teaspoon dried thyme
  leaves
2 (8-ounce) packages
  refrigerated crescent
  dinner roll dough
1 egg, beaten
  Sesame or poppy seed

In large skillet, over medium heat, cook sausage, mushrooms and onion until
sausage is cooked, stirring occasionally to break up sausage. Remove from heat.
Stir in cheese, mustard, bell pepper and thyme.

Separate each package of dough into 4 rectangles; press perforations together to
seal. On floured surface, roll each rectangle into 6-inch square. Cut each square
into quarters, making 32 squares total. Place 1 scant tablespoon sausage mixture
on each square; fold dough over filling on the diagonal to form triangle. Press
edges with fork to seal. Place on greased baking sheets.

Brush triangles with beaten egg and sprinkle with sesame or poppy seed. Bake
at 375°F for 10 to 12 minutes or until golden brown. Serve warm.

Savory Sausage Mushroom
Turnovers

SPIRAL REUBEN DIJON BITES

Makes 32 appetizers

1 sheet puff pastry
 (½ package)
¼ cup GREY POUPON
 Dijon Mustard
6 slices Swiss cheese
 (3 ounces)
6 slices deli corned beef
 (6 ounces)

1 egg, beaten
1 tablespoon caraway seed
 Additional GREY
 POUPON Dijon
 Mustard

Thaw puff pastry sheet according to package directions. Roll puff pastry dough to 12×10-inch rectangle. Spread mustard evenly over dough; top with cheese and corned beef. Cut in half crosswise to form 2 (10×6-inch) rectangles. Roll up each rectangle from short end, jelly-roll fashion; pinch seams to seal.*

Cut each roll into 16 (¼-inch-thick) slices. Place slices, cut-sides up, on lightly greased baking sheets; brush with beaten egg and sprinkle with caraway seed. Bake at 400°F for 10 to 12 minutes or until golden. Serve warm with additional mustard.

*Rolls may be wrapped and frozen. To serve, thaw at room temperature for 30 minutes. Slice and bake as directed above.

EASY CHEDDAR MUSTARD BEER DIP

Makes 2½ cups

12 ounces pasteurized
 processed Cheddar
 cheese spread, cubed
4 ounces cream cheese,
 cubed
⅔ cup beer
½ cup GREY POUPON
 Dijon Mustard

⅓ cup chopped green onions
 Chopped red bell pepper,
 for garnish
 Pretzel chips, breadsticks
 or bagel chips, for
 dipping

In medium saucepan, over low heat, heat cheese spread and cream cheese until melted and smooth. Slowly blend in beer and mustard. Stir in green onions. Pour into serving bowl; garnish with chopped bell pepper. Serve with pretzel chips, breadsticks or bagel chips.

Spiral Rueben Dijon Bites

☗ GREY ☗ POUPON®

SOUPS & SALADS

MIXED SALAD WITH RASPBERRY HONEY DIJON DRESSING

Makes 6 servings

⅓ cup **GREY POUPON COUNTRY DIJON Mustard***
⅓ cup **dairy sour cream****
¼ cup **raspberry-flavored vinegar**
2 tablespoons **honey***
4 cups **mixed salad greens**

1 cup **cut green beans, steamed**
1 cup **cooked sliced beets**
½ cup **sliced mushrooms**
½ cup **shredded carrots**
8 ounces **turkey, cut into julienne strips**

In small bowl, combine mustard, sour cream, vinegar and honey; chill dressing until serving time.

On large serving platter lined with salad greens, arrange vegetables and turkey. Drizzle with prepared dressing just before serving.

*⅓ cup Grey Poupon Honey Mustard may be substituted for Country Dijon mustard; omit honey.

**Lowfat sour cream may be substituted for regular sour cream.

Mixed Salad with Raspberry Honey Dijon Dressing

RAVIOLI SOUP

Makes 8 servings

8 ounces sweet Italian sausage, casing removed
1 clove garlic, crushed
2 (13¾-fluid ounce) cans lower sodium chicken broth
2 cups water
1 (9-ounce) package frozen miniature cheese-filled ravioli
1 (15-ounce) can garbanzo beans, drained
1 (14½-ounce) can stewed tomatoes
⅓ cup GREY POUPON Dijon Mustard
½ teaspoon dried oregano leaves
¼ teaspoon coarsely ground black pepper
1 cup torn fresh spinach leaves
Grated Parmesan cheese

In 4-quart heavy pot, over medium heat, brown sausage and cook garlic until tender, stirring to break up sausage, about 5 minutes. Pour off excess fat; remove sausage mixture from pot and set aside.

In same pot, over medium-high heat, heat chicken broth and water to a boil. Add ravioli; cook for 4 to 5 minutes or until tender. Stir in beans, stewed tomatoes, sausage mixture, mustard, oregano and pepper; heat through. Stir in spinach and cook until wilted, about 1 minute. Serve topped with Parmesan cheese.

CURRIED CHICKEN SALAD

Makes 4 servings

2 cups cubed cooked chicken
1 cup diced celery
1 cup sliced green onions
½ cup GREY POUPON Dijon Mustard
¼ cup chutney
2 tablespoons olive oil
1½ teaspoons curry powder
¼ teaspoon salt
¼ teaspoon coarsely ground black pepper
Mixed salad greens

In large bowl, combine chicken, celery and green onions. In small bowl, whisk mustard, chutney, oil, curry powder, salt and pepper until well blended. Pour over chicken mixture, tossing to coat well. Chill at least 1 hour. Serve on bed of salad greens.

Ravioli Soup

SANTA FE BLACK BEANS & RICE SALAD

Makes 6 cups

½ cup GREY POUPON Dijon Mustard

2 tablespoons Regina® White Wine Vinegar

2 tablespoons olive oil

1 tablespoon chopped cilantro

1½ teaspoons liquid hot pepper seasoning

½ teaspoon chili powder

¼ teaspoon ground cumin

3 cups cooked long grain and wild rice

1 (15-ounce) can black beans, rinsed and drained

1 cup chopped tomato

1 cup canned corn

⅓ cup chopped red onion

¼ cup Ortega® Diced Green Chiles

In small bowl, blend mustard, vinegar, oil, cilantro, hot pepper seasoning, chili powder and cumin; set aside.

In large bowl, combine rice, beans, tomato, corn, onion and chiles. Add mustard mixture, tossing to coat well. Chill at least 1 hour before serving. Garnish as desired.

CREAMY DIJON COLESLAW

Makes about 5 cups

½ cup GREY POUPON COUNTRY DIJON Mustard

½ cup prepared ranch, creamy Italian or blue cheese salad dressing

2 tablespoons chopped parsley

½ teaspoon celery seed

3 cups shredded green cabbage

2 cups shredded red cabbage

1 cup shredded carrots

½ cup chopped onion

⅓ cup chopped red bell pepper

In small bowl, blend mustard, salad dressing, parsley and celery seed; set aside.

In large bowl, combine green and red cabbages, carrots, onion and bell pepper. Add mustard mixture, tossing to coat well. Chill at least 1 hour before serving.

Santa Fe Black Beans & Rice Salad

GRILLED CHICKEN CAESAR SALAD

Makes 6 servings

½ cup olive oil
¼ cup **GREY POUPON COUNTRY DIJON** Mustard
2 tablespoons lemon juice
2 teaspoons Worcestershire sauce
1 teaspoon grated lemon peel
1 clove garlic, minced
½ teaspoon sugar

¼ teaspoon coarsely ground black pepper
1 pound boneless, skinless chicken breasts
5 cups torn Romaine lettuce
1 cup sliced mushrooms
1 cup cherry tomato halves
½ cup prepared seasoned croutons
1 tablespoon grated Parmesan cheese

In small bowl, whisk together oil, mustard, lemon juice, Worcestershire sauce, lemon peel, garlic, sugar and pepper. In nonmetal bowl, pour ¼ cup mustard dressing over chicken breasts, turning to coat. Cover and chill at least 1 hour. Chill remaining dressing until serving time.

Remove chicken from marinade; discard marinade. Grill or broil chicken breasts for 10 to 15 minutes or until done, turning once. Diagonally slice chicken breasts into strips.

In large bowl, combine lettuce, chicken, mushrooms, tomatoes and croutons. Toss with reserved dressing; sprinkle with Parmesan cheese and serve.

Grilled Chicken Caesar Salad

MARINATED VEGETABLES

Makes 6 servings

2 cups broccoli flowerettes
2 cups cauliflower
    flowerettes
8 ounces fresh green beans,
    cut into 2-inch pieces
2 cups diagonally sliced
    carrots
1 cup cherry tomatoes,
    halved
½ cup chopped red onion
⅓ cup GREY POUPON
    COUNTRY DIJON
    Mustard

⅓ cup olive oil
¼ cup Regina® Red Wine
    Vinegar
1 teaspoon sugar
1 teaspoon dried oregano
    leaves
¼ teaspoon coarsely ground
    black pepper
⅓ cup oil-packed sundried
    tomato strips

In large heavy pot, steam broccoli, cauliflower, green beans and carrots until tender-crisp. Rinse vegetables in cold water and drain well; place in large serving bowl. Stir in cherry tomatoes and onion.

In small bowl, whisk mustard, oil, vinegar, sugar, oregano and pepper; stir in sundried tomatoes. Pour dressing over vegetables, tossing to coat well. Chill for at least 2 hours before serving, stirring occasionally. Garnish as desired.

DIJON HAM AND LENTIL SOUP

Makes 6 servings

1 cup finely chopped onion
¾ cup finely chopped green
    bell pepper
½ cup finely chopped carrot
1 clove garlic, minced
1 bay leaf
2 (13¾-fluid ounce) cans
    chicken broth or lower
    sodium chicken broth

1 (14½-ounce) can stewed
    tomatoes
1¼ cups water
1 cup diced ham
¾ cup dry lentils
½ cup GREY POUPON
    COUNTRY DIJON
    Mustard

In large saucepan, combine all ingredients except mustard. Heat to a boil over medium-high heat. Reduce heat; simmer, uncovered, for 1 hour. Stir in mustard. Serve hot.

Marinated Vegetables

MEDITERRANEAN COUSCOUS

Makes 6 servings

1 (10-ounce) package
  couscous
⅓ cup GREY POUPON
  COUNTRY DIJON
  Mustard
¼ cup lemon juice
¼ cup chopped parsley
3 tablespoons chopped fresh
  mint
1 tablespoon grated lemon
  peel

1 clove garlic, minced
⅔ cup olive oil
4 ounces feta cheese, diced
½ cup chopped pitted ripe
  olives
1 (7-ounce) jar roasted red
  peppers, drained and
  chopped
Sliced tomatoes and
  cucumbers, for garnish

Prepare couscous according to package directions; cool.

In small bowl, whisk mustard, lemon juice, parsley, mint, lemon peel and garlic until blended. Whisk in oil.

In large bowl, combine couscous, cheese, olives and peppers; add mustard mixture, tossing to coat well. Chill at least 1 hour. To serve, arrange couscous mixture on serving plate; garnish with tomato and cucumber slices.

GRILLED CHICKEN SALAD WITH AVOCADO DRESSING

Makes 6 servings

1 cup vegetable oil
⅓ cup GREY POUPON
  Dijon Mustard
¼ cup Regina® Red Wine
  Vinegar
2 tablespoons lime juice
2 tablespoons chopped
  cilantro or parsley
¼ teaspoon dried oregano
  leaves

⅛ teaspoon ground red
  pepper
6 boneless, skinless
  chicken breasts
  (about 1½ pounds)
1 ripe medium avocado,
  pitted and peeled
6 cups torn salad greens
1 large tomato, cut into
  wedges

In small bowl, whisk oil, mustard, vinegar, lime juice, cilantro or parsley, oregano and pepper until blended. Reserve 1 cup mustard mixture. In nonmetal dish, combine remaining mustard mixture and chicken. Cover; chill for at least 2 hours.

In blender or food processor, blend avocado and 1 cup reserved mustard mixture until smooth. Cover; chill until serving time.

Remove chicken from marinade, reserving marinade. Grill or broil chicken 6 inches from heat source for 10 to 15 minutes or until done, turning and brushing with marinade occasionally. Slice chicken on a diagonal. Serve chicken on salad greens; top with tomato and avocado dressing.

CHINATOWN TURKEY SALAD

Makes 6 servings

⅓ cup **GREY POUPON Dijon Mustard***
¼ cup **orange juice**
¼ cup **chopped green onions**
2 tablespoons **vegetable oil**
2 tablespoons **honey***
1 tablespoon **soy sauce**
½ teaspoon **grated fresh ginger**
4 cups **mixed salad greens**
1½ cups **blanched pea pods**

1 (11-ounce) can **mandarin orange segments, drained**
1 (5-ounce) can **sliced water chestnuts, drained**
8 ounces **deli smoked turkey breast, cut into julienne strips**
1 cup **crispy Chinese noodles**

In small saucepan, over medium heat, heat mustard, orange juice, green onions, oil, honey, soy sauce and ginger for 2 to 3 minutes or until heated through; keep warm.

On large serving platter, layer salad greens, pea pods, orange segments, water chestnuts, turkey strips and noodles. Serve salad drizzled with warm mustard dressing.

*⅓ cup Grey Poupon Honey Mustard may be substituted for Dijon mustard; omit honey.

VEGETABLE AND SHRIMP CHOWDER

Makes 8 servings

1½ cups diced Spanish onions
½ cup sliced carrots
½ cup diced celery
2 tablespoons margarine or butter
2 cups peeled and diced baking potatoes
1 (10-ounce) package frozen corn

5 cups chicken broth or lower sodium chicken broth
½ pound small shrimp, peeled and deveined
⅓ cup GREY POUPON Dijon Mustard
¼ cup chopped parsley

In large saucepan, over medium heat, cook onions, carrots and celery in margarine or butter for 3 to 4 minutes or until tender. Add potatoes, corn and chicken broth; heat to a boil. Reduce heat; simmer for 20 to 25 minutes or until potatoes are tender. Add shrimp, mustard and parsley; cook for 5 minutes more or until shrimp are cooked. Garnish as desired. Serve warm.

COUNTRY BACON POTATO SALAD

Makes 5 servings

2 pounds red potatoes, cooked, peeled and diced
½ cup chopped green, red or yellow bell pepper
1 small red onion, thinly sliced
6 slices bacon, cooked and crumbled
⅓ cup mayonnaise*

⅓ cup GREY POUPON Dijon Mustard
2 tablespoons Regina® Red Wine Vinegar
½ teaspoon garlic powder
2 tablespoons chopped parsley
½ teaspoon dried oregano leaves

In large bowl, combine potatoes, bell pepper, onion and bacon; set aside.

In small bowl, blend remaining ingredients; stir into potato mixture, tossing to coat well. Cover; chill at least 2 hours to blend flavors.

Lowfat mayonnaise may be substituted for regular mayonnaise.

Vegetable and Shrimp Chowder

CONFETTI BARLEY SALAD

4 cups water
1 cup dry pearl barley
⅓ cup GREY POUPON Dijon Mustard
⅓ cup olive oil
¼ cup Regina® Red Wine Vinegar
2 tablespoons chopped parsley
2 teaspoons chopped fresh rosemary leaves *or* ½ teaspoon dried rosemary leaves

2 teaspoons grated orange peel
1 teaspoon sugar
1½ cups diced red, green or yellow bell peppers
½ cup sliced green onions
½ cup sliced pitted ripe olives
Fresh rosemary and orange and tomato slices, for garnish

In 3-quart saucepan, over medium-high heat, heat water and barley to a boil; reduce heat. Cover; simmer for 45 to 55 minutes or until tender. Drain and cool.

In small bowl, whisk mustard, oil, vinegar, parsley, rosemary, orange peel and sugar until blended; set aside.

In large bowl, combine barley, bell peppers, green onions and olives. Stir in mustard dressing, tossing to coat well. Chill several hours to blend flavors. To serve, spoon barley mixture onto serving platter; garnish with rosemary and orange and tomato slices.

Confetti Barley Salad

ROSEMARY LEMON CHICKEN SALAD

Makes 4 servings

2 cups cubed cooked
  chicken
1 cup chopped onions
1 cup diced celery
½ cup chopped roasted red
  pepper
⅓ cup GREY POUPON
  COUNTRY DIJON
  Mustard

¼ cup olive oil
2 tablespoons lemon juice
1½ teaspoons dried rosemary
  leaves
1 teaspoon grated lemon
  peel
½ teaspoon coarsely ground
  black pepper
¼ teaspoon salt

In large bowl, combine chicken, onions, celery and roasted red pepper. In small bowl, whisk mustard, oil, lemon juice, rosemary, lemon peel, black pepper and salt until blended. Pour over chicken mixture, tossing to coat well. Chill at least 1 hour. Serve as a salad or sandwich filling. Garnish as desired.

DIJON ROASTED VEGETABLE SOUP

Makes 8 servings

2 plum tomatoes, halved
1 medium zucchini, split
  lengthwise and halved
1 large onion, quartered
1 red bell pepper, sliced
1 cup sliced carrots
2 to 3 cloves garlic
5 cups chicken broth or
  lower sodium chicken
  broth

¼ teaspoon ground cumin
¼ teaspoon crushed red
  pepper flakes
2 cups diced cooked chicken
  (about 10 ounces)
½ cup GREY POUPON
  Dijon Mustard
¼ cup chopped parsley

On large baking sheet, arrange tomatoes, zucchini, onion, bell pepper, carrots and garlic. Bake at 325°F for 30 to 45 minutes or until golden and tender. Remove from oven and cool. Chop vegetables.

In 3-quart pot, over high heat, heat chicken broth, chopped vegetables, cumin and red pepper flakes to a boil; reduce heat. Simmer for 5 minutes. Stir in chicken and mustard; cook for 5 minutes more. Stir in parsley and serve warm.

Rosemary Lemon Chicken Salad

❧ GREY ❧ POUPON®

SANDWICHES & SIDES

DIJON BACON CHEESEBURGERS

Makes 4 burgers

1 cup shredded Cheddar cheese (4 ounces)
5 tablespoons GREY POUPON Dijon Mustard,* divided
2 teaspoons dried minced onion
1 teaspoon prepared horseradish*

1 pound lean ground beef
4 onion sandwich rolls, split and toasted
1 cup shredded lettuce
4 slices tomato
4 slices bacon, cooked and halved

In small bowl, combine cheese, 3 tablespoons mustard, onion and horseradish; set aside.

In medium bowl, combine ground beef and remaining mustard; shape mixture into 4 patties. Grill or broil burgers over medium heat for 5 minutes on each side or until desired doneness; top with cheese mixture and cook until cheese melts, about 2 minutes. Top each roll bottom with ¼ cup shredded lettuce, 1 tomato slice, burger, 2 bacon pieces and roll top. Serve immediately.

5 tablespoons Grey Poupon Horseradish Mustard may be substituted for Dijon mustard; omit horseradish.

Dijon Bacon Cheeseburger

MACARONI AND CHEESE DIJON

Makes 6 servings

1¼ cups milk
12 ounces pasteurized process
  Cheddar cheese spread,
  cubed
½ cup GREY POUPON
  Dijon Mustard
⅓ cup sliced green onions
6 slices bacon, cooked and
  crumbled

⅛ teaspoon ground red
  pepper
12 ounces tri-color rotelle or
  spiral-shaped pasta,
  cooked
1 (2.8-ounce) can French
  fried onion rings

In medium saucepan, over low heat, heat milk, cheese and mustard until cheese melts and mixture is smooth. Stir in green onions, bacon and pepper; remove from heat.

In large bowl, combine hot pasta and cheese mixture, tossing until well coated; spoon into greased 2-quart casserole. Cover; bake at 350°F for 15 to 20 minutes. Uncover and stir; top with onion rings. Bake, uncovered, for 5 minutes more. Let stand 10 minutes before serving. Garnish as desired.

CALIFORNIA HAM AND CHEESE PITAS

Makes 5 servings

2 cups chopped honey-
  baked ham
1 cup shredded Cheddar
  cheese (4 ounces)
½ cup chopped red or green
  bell pepper
⅓ cup GREY POUPON
  COUNTRY DIJON
  Mustard

⅓ cup lowfat plain yogurt
1 tablespoon chopped
  cilantro
5 (6-inch) whole wheat pita
  breads, split open
1¼ cups alfalfa sprouts
2 small tomatoes, sliced
1 ripe medium avocado,
  peeled, pitted and sliced

In small bowl, combine ham, cheese, bell pepper, mustard, yogurt and cilantro. Chill until serving time.

To serve, line each pita with ¼ cup sprouts, tomato and avocado slices; spoon ham filling into pitas. Serve immediately.

Macaroni and Cheese Dijon

SMOKED TURKEY AND PROVOLONE CROISSANTS

Makes 4 sandwiches

⅓ cup GREY POUPON
   COUNTRY DIJON
   Mustard
2 tablespoons mayonnaise*
1 tablespoon chopped fresh
   basil leaves
4 croissants, split
   horizontally
1 cup fresh spinach leaves

6 ounces deli sliced smoked
   turkey breast
1 small red onion, thinly
   sliced
4 ounces deli sliced
   Provolone cheese
1 medium tomato, thinly
   sliced

In small bowl, blend mustard, mayonnaise and basil. Spread mustard mixture on cut sides of each croissant. Layer spinach leaves, turkey, onion, cheese and tomato on croissant bottoms; replace croissant tops. Serve immediately.

Lowfat mayonnaise may be substituted for regular mayonnaise.

DIJON GARLIC HERB LOAF

Makes 16 servings

2 cloves garlic, minced
⅓ cup margarine or butter
⅓ cup GREY POUPON
   Dijon Mustard
1 tablespoon minced chives

1 teaspoon dried oregano
   leaves
1 (16-inch) loaf Italian bread
¼ cup grated Parmesan
   cheese

In skillet, over medium heat, sauté garlic in margarine or butter until lightly browned; remove from heat. Stir in mustard, chives and oregano. Slice bread crosswise into 16 slices, cutting ¾ of the way through. Brush mustard mixture on cut sides of bread; sprinkle with cheese. Wrap loaf in foil. Bake at 400°F for 15 to 20 minutes or until heated through. Remove bread from foil; break apart to serve.

*Smoked Turkey and
Provolone Croissant*

ROASTED GARLIC MASHED POTATOES

1 large bulb garlic
  Olive oil
¼ cup chopped green onions
¼ cup margarine or butter
2½ pounds potatoes, peeled,
  cubed and cooked
1½ cups milk

½ cup GREY POUPON
  Dijon Mustard
½ cup shredded Cheddar
  cheese (2 ounces)
¼ cup chopped parsley
  Salt and pepper, to taste

To roast garlic, peel off loose paperlike skin from bulb. Coat garlic bulb lightly with olive oil; wrap in foil. Place in small baking pan. Bake at 400°F for 40 to 45 minutes; cool. Separate cloves. Squeeze cloves to extract pulp; discard skins.

In large saucepan, over medium heat, sauté garlic pulp and green onions in margarine or butter until tender. Add cooked potatoes, milk, mustard and cheese. Mash potato mixture until smooth and well blended. Stir in parsley; season with salt and pepper. Serve immediately.

HOT DOGS WITH DIJON KRAUT

1 (14-ounce) can sauerkraut
¼ cup GREY POUPON
  Dijon Mustard
¼ cup prepared barbecue
  sauce
⅓ cup chopped onion
1 tablespoon sweet pickle
  relish

1 teaspoon caraway seed
6 hot dogs, grilled
6 oblong sandwich buns or
  hot dog rolls, toasted
1½ cups shredded Cheddar
  cheese (6 ounces)

In medium saucepan, over medium heat, heat sauerkraut, mustard, barbecue sauce, onion, pickle relish and caraway seed to a boil; reduce heat. Cover; simmer for 2 minutes. Keep warm.

Place hot dogs in buns; top each with ¼ cup cheese. Broil for 1 minute or until cheese melts. Top with sauerkraut mixture and serve immediately.

MEDITERRANEAN BURGERS

Makes 4 burgers

½ cup crumbled feta cheese (3 ounces)

5 tablespoons GREY POUPON COUNTRY DIJON Mustard, divided

2 tablespoons mayonnaise*

2 tablespoons sliced ripe olives

2 tablespoons diced pimientos

1 pound lean ground beef

4 sesame seed sandwich rolls, split and toasted

4 Bibb lettuce leaves

4 thin slices red onion

In small bowl, combine cheese, 3 tablespoons mustard, mayonnaise, olives and pimientos; set aside.

In medium bowl, combine ground beef and remaining mustard; shape mixture into 4 patties. Grill or broil burgers over medium heat for 5 minutes on each side or until desired doneness. Top each roll bottom with 1 lettuce leaf, 1 tablespoon cheese mixture, burger, 1 onion slice, 1 tablespoon cheese mixture and roll top. Serve immediately.

Lowfat mayonnaise may be substituted for regular mayonnaise.

EGGPLANT & PEPPER CHEESE SANDWICHES

Makes 6 sandwiches

1 (8-ounce) eggplant, cut
    into 18 slices
Salt and pepper, to taste
⅓ cup GREY POUPON
    COUNTRY DIJON
    Mustard
¼ cup olive oil
2 tablespoons Regina® Red
    Wine Vinegar

¾ teaspoon dried oregano
    leaves
1 clove garlic, crushed
6 (4-inch) pieces French
    bread, cut in half
1 (7-ounce) jar roasted red
    peppers, cut into strips
1½ cups shredded mozzarella
    cheese (6 ounces)

Place eggplant slices on greased baking sheet, overlapping slightly. Sprinkle lightly with salt and pepper. Bake at 400°F for 10 to 12 minutes or until tender.

Blend mustard, oil, vinegar, oregano and garlic. Brush eggplant slices with ¼ cup mustard mixture; broil eggplant for 1 minute.

Brush cut sides of French bread with remaining mustard mixture. Layer 3 slices eggplant, a few red pepper strips and ¼ cup cheese on each bread bottom. Place on broiler pan with roll tops, cut-sides up; broil until cheese melts. Close sandwiches with bread tops and serve immediately; garnish as desired.

Eggplant & Pepper
Cheese Sandwich

HAM AND SWISS SANDWICHES WITH CITRUS MAYONNAISE

Makes 4 sandwiches

¼ cup GREY POUPON
  Dijon Mustard
¼ cup mayonnaise*
1 tablespoon lime juice
1 tablespoon honey
½ teaspoon grated lime peel
¼ teaspoon ground black
  pepper

8 (½-inch-thick) slices
  black bread
1 cup shredded lettuce
8 slices tomato
4 ounces sliced Swiss cheese
12 ounces sliced honey-baked
  ham

In small bowl, blend mustard, mayonnaise, lime juice, honey, lime peel and pepper. Spread about 1 tablespoon mustard mixture on each bread slice. On each of 4 bread slices, layer ¼ cup lettuce, 2 tomato slices, 1 ounce cheese and 3 ounces ham. Top with remaining bread slices. Serve with remaining mustard mixture.

Lowfat mayonnaise may be substituted for regular mayonnaise.

*Ham and Swiss Sandwich with
Citrus Mayonnaise*

GRILLED COUNTRY DIJON VEGETABLES

Makes 6 to 8 servings

⅓ cup GREY POUPON
   COUNTRY DIJON
   Mustard
⅓ cup olive oil
¼ cup balsamic vinegar
¼ cup chopped parsley
2 tablespoons chopped
   chives

1 tablespoon minced garlic
4 baby eggplants
2 Spanish onions
2 medium zucchini
2 medium yellow squash
2 roasted red peppers, cut
   into strips

In bowl, whisk mustard, oil, vinegar, parsley, chives and garlic until blended; set aside.

Cut each eggplant and onion crosswise into 4 slices; cut zucchini and yellow squash into 8 slices. Grill vegetables, basting with ¾ cup mustard mixture. Grill onions for about 6 to 8 minutes and remaining vegetables for 2 to 3 minutes. To serve, arrange vegetables on serving platter; top with pepper strips and drizzle with remaining mustard mixture.

ITALIAN SUBS

Makes 6 to 8 servings

½ cup prepared Italian salad
   dressing
¼ cup GREY POUPON
   Dijon Mustard
1 teaspoon dried oregano
   leaves
1 (18- to 20-inch) loaf
   Italian bread, split
   lengthwise

2 cups shredded lettuce
8 ounces deli sliced ham
4 ounces deli sliced salami
1 (7-ounce) jar roasted red
   peppers, cut into strips
4 ounces deli sliced
   Provolone cheese
1 small red onion, thinly
   sliced

In small bowl, whisk salad dressing, mustard and oregano until blended. Spread dressing mixture over cut sides of bread. Place half the lettuce on bottom half of bread; top with layers of ham, salami, pepper strips, cheese, onion and remaining lettuce. Replace bread top; slice and serve.

Grilled Country Dijon Vegetables

REUBEN DIJON

Makes 4 sandwiches

¼ cup GREY POUPON
   COUNTRY DIJON
   Mustard
¼ cup mayonnaise*
2 tablespoons chili sauce
1 tablespoon sweet pickle
   relish

8 slices seeded rye bread
4 ounces sliced Swiss cheese
8 ounces sliced deli corned
   beef
½ cup sauerkraut
2 tablespoons margarine or
   butter, softened

In small bowl, blend mustard, mayonnaise, chili sauce and pickle relish. Spread mixture on each bread slice. Layer 1 ounce cheese, 2 ounces corned beef and 2 tablespoons sauerkraut on each of 4 bread slices; top with remaining bread slices to form sandwiches. Spread outside of each sandwich with margarine or butter. In large skillet or griddle, over medium heat, brown sandwiches on each side until cheese melts, about 3 to 4 minutes. Cut sandwiches in half and serve immediately.

Lowfat mayonnaise may be substituted for regular mayonnaise.

MIXED VEGETABLE SAUCEPAN STUFFING

Makes 5 servings

½ cup *each* chopped onion,
   celery, carrot and
   mushrooms
2 tablespoons margarine or
   butter
1 (13¾-fluid ounce) can
   lower sodium chicken
   broth
⅓ cup GREY POUPON
   COUNTRY DIJON
   Mustard

½ teaspoon poultry seasoning
¼ teaspoon rosemary leaves
5 cups dried bread stuffing
   cubes
⅓ cup Planters® Walnuts,
   chopped
2 tablespoons chopped
   parsley

In large saucepan, over medium-high heat, sauté onion, celery, carrot and mushrooms in margarine or butter until tender. Stir in chicken broth, mustard, poultry seasoning and rosemary. Heat mixture to a boil; reduce heat. Cover and simmer for 5 minutes. Add bread cubes, walnuts and parsley, stirring to coat well. Cover; let stand for 5 minutes. Fluff with fork before serving.

GRILLED CHICKEN SANDWICHES MONTEREY

Makes 4 sandwiches

⅓ cup dairy sour cream*
⅓ cup Ortega® Thick &
  Chunky Salsa
¼ cup GREY POUPON
  Dijon Mustard, divided
4 boneless, skinless chicken
  breasts, pounded slightly
  (about 1 pound)

8 slices Muenster cheese
  (4 ounces)
4 croissants
1 cup shredded lettuce
8 slices tomato
4 slices ripe avocado

In small bowl, blend sour cream, salsa and 2 tablespoons mustard; set sauce aside.

Grill or broil chicken for 8 to 10 minutes or until done, turning and brushing with remaining mustard. Top each breast with 2 slices cheese; cook 1 minute more or until cheese melts.

Cut croissants in half; spread cut sides with ¼ cup prepared sauce. Place ¼ cup lettuce on each croissant bottom; top with chicken breast, 2 tomato slices, 1 avocado slice and croissant top. Serve with remaining sauce.

Lowfat sour cream may be substituted for regular sour cream.

ONION & PEPPER CHEESESTEAKS

Makes 4 servings

2 medium onions, thinly
    sliced
1 cup red, yellow and/or
    green bell pepper strips
2 tablespoons margarine or
    butter
½ cup GREY POUPON
    Dijon Mustard, divided

1 tablespoon honey
4 (6- to 8-inch) steak rolls
8 frozen sandwich steaks,
    cooked
1 cup shredded Cheddar
    cheese (4 ounces)

In large skillet, over medium-high heat, sauté onions and bell pepper in margarine or butter until tender. Stir in 6 tablespoons mustard and honey; reduce heat and cook 2 minutes. Keep warm.

Cut rolls in half lengthwise, not cutting completely through rolls; brush cut sides of rolls with remaining mustard. Broil rolls, cut-sides up, until golden. Top each roll with cooked steaks, onion mixture and cheese. Broil for 1 minute more or until cheese melts. Close sandwiches and serve immediately.

Onion & Pepper Cheesesteak

⚜ GREY ⚜ POUPON®

ENTRÉES

PESTO DIJON PIZZA

Makes 4 main-dish or 8 appetizer servings

½ cup chopped parsley*
⅓ cup GREY POUPON
  Dijon Mustard
¼ cup Planters® Walnuts,
  chopped*
1 tablespoon olive oil*
2 tablespoons grated
  Parmesan cheese,*
  divided

1½ teaspoons dried basil
  leaves,* divided
2 (8-ounce) packages small
  prepared pizza crusts
4 ounces thinly sliced deli
  baked ham
3 plum tomatoes, sliced
1 cup shredded mozzarella
  cheese (4 ounces)

In small bowl, combine parsley, mustard, walnuts, oil, 1 tablespoon Parmesan cheese and 1 teaspoon basil. Divide mixture and spread evenly onto each pizza crust. Top each crust with 2 ounces ham, tomato slices and mozzarella cheese. Sprinkle with remaining Parmesan cheese and basil. Place on baking sheet. Bake at 450°F for 8 to 10 minutes or until cheese melts. Cut into wedges; serve warm.

1 (7-ounce) container prepared pesto sauce may be substituted for parsley, walnuts, olive oil, 1 tablespoon Parmesan cheese and 1 teaspoon basil. Stir mustard into prepared pesto sauce.

Pesto Dijon Pizza

Makes 6 servings

1 cup chopped onions
1 clove garlic, minced
1 tablespoon vegetable oil
1 pound ground turkey
1 cup chicken broth or lower sodium chicken broth
1 (14½-ounce) can stewed tomatoes
⅓ cup GREY POUPON Dijon Mustard

1 tablespoon chili powder
⅛ to ¼ teaspoon ground red pepper
1 (15-ounce) can cannellini beans, drained and rinsed
1 (8-ounce) can corn, drained
Tortilla chips, shredded Cheddar cheese and cilantro, optional

In 3-quart saucepan, over medium-high heat, sauté onions and garlic in oil until tender. Add turkey; cook until done, stirring occasionally to break up meat. Drain. Stir in chicken broth, tomatoes, mustard, chili powder and pepper. Heat to a boil; reduce heat. Simmer for 10 minutes. Stir in beans and corn; cook for 5 minutes. Top with tortilla chips, shredded cheese and cilantro if desired.

20-Minute White Bean Chili

GRILLED BEEF WITH TWO SAUCES

Makes 4 servings

1 (1-pound) boneless beef sirloin steak

ROASTED GARLIC SAUCE
¾ cup mayonnaise*
¼ cup Roasted Garlic Purée
  (recipe follows)
¼ cup GREY POUPON
  Dijon Mustard
1 tablespoon lemon juice
2 tablespoons chopped
  parsley

SUNDRIED TOMATO SAUCE
¾ cup chopped roasted red
  peppers
½ cup sundried tomatoes,**
  chopped
3 tablespoons GREY
  POUPON Dijon
  Mustard
2 tablespoons chopped
  parsley
2 to 3 tablespoons olive oil
¼ teaspoon crushed red
  pepper flakes

Grill beef over medium heat to desired doneness and chill.

For Roasted Garlic Sauce, in medium bowl, blend all ingredients. Chill at least 1 hour to blend flavors.

For Sundried Tomato Sauce, in medium bowl, combine roasted red peppers, sundried tomatoes, mustard and parsley. Slowly add oil as needed to bind. Add red pepper flakes. Chill at least 1 hour to blend flavors. Bring to room temperature before serving.

To serve, slice beef and arrange on 4 serving plates. Spoon about 2 tablespoons of each sauce onto each plate. Serve with sliced tomatoes and cooled steamed asparagus; garnish as desired.

Lowfat mayonnaise may be substituted for regular mayonnaise.

**If sundried tomatoes are very dry, soften in warm water for 15 minutes. Drain before using.*

ROASTED GARLIC PURÉE: Remove excess papery outside of 1 head garlic and separate into cloves. Place in 8×8×2-inch baking pan. Add 2 to 3 tablespoons olive oil and 1 cup chicken broth. Bake at 350°F for 25 to 30 minutes or until garlic is soft. Cool and squeeze garlic pulp from skins; discard liquid in pan.

Grilled Beef with Two Sauces

SPINACH MEATLOAF DIJON

Makes 6 to 8 servings

1½ pounds lean ground beef
¾ cup plain dry bread crumbs
½ cup GREY POUPON Dijon Mustard, divided
2 eggs
1 (10-ounce) package frozen chopped spinach, thawed and well drained

1 cup shredded Swiss cheese (4 ounces)
½ cup minced onion
2 teaspoons chopped fresh dill weed
1 teaspoon coarsely ground black pepper
1 clove garlic, minced
2 tablespoons honey

In large bowl, combine ground beef, bread crumbs, 5 tablespoons mustard, eggs, spinach, cheese, onion, dill, pepper and garlic. Shape mixture into 9×5-inch loaf; place in greased 13×9×2-inch baking pan. Bake at 350°F for 60 to 70 minutes or until done. Blend remaining mustard and honey; brush on meatloaf during last 10 minutes of baking time. Remove from oven and let stand 10 minutes. Slice and serve.

PORK TENDERLOIN WITH PEACH MANGO CHUTNEY

Makes 6 servings

⅔ cup GREY POUPON COUNTRY DIJON Mustard
½ cup peach preserves
1 tablespoon cider vinegar
2 teaspoons chopped chives
½ cup chopped celery
1 clove garlic, minced

1 tablespoon vegetable oil
½ cup chopped mango
¼ cup dark seedless raisins
1 tablespoon chopped parsley
2 pork tenderloins (¾ pound each)

In small bowl, blend mustard, preserves, vinegar and chives. Set aside ⅓ cup mixture for glazing pork tenderloins.

In small saucepan, over medium-high heat, sauté celery and garlic in oil until tender. Stir in remaining mustard mixture; cook 2 minutes. Remove from heat; cool slightly. Stir in mango, raisins and parsley; set aside.

Place tenderloins on rack in roasting pan. Roast pork at 450°F for 10 minutes. Reduce to 350°F and bake 30 to 35 minutes or until done. Brush pork with reserved mustard mixture during last 15 minutes of roasting. Slice pork and serve with mango chutney.

THAI PEANUT NOODLE STIR-FRY

Makes 4 to 6 servings

1 cup chicken broth or
lower sodium chicken
broth
½ cup GREY POUPON
Dijon Mustard
⅓ cup creamy peanut butter
3 tablespoons firmly packed
light brown sugar
2 tablespoons soy sauce
1 clove garlic, crushed
½ teaspoon minced fresh
ginger

1 tablespoon cornstarch
4 cups cut-up vegetables
(red pepper, carrot,
mushrooms, green
onions, pea pods)
1 tablespoon vegetable oil
1 pound linguine, cooked
Chopped peanuts and
scallion brushes, for
garnish

In medium saucepan, combine chicken broth, mustard, peanut butter, sugar, soy sauce, garlic, ginger and cornstarch. Cook over medium heat until mixture thickens and begins to boil; reduce heat and keep warm.

In large skillet, over medium-high heat, sauté vegetables in oil until tender, about 5 minutes. In large serving bowl, combine hot cooked pasta, vegetables and peanut sauce, tossing until well coated. Garnish with chopped peanuts and scallion brushes. Serve immediately.

PENNE PRIMAVERA WITH SUNDRIED TOMATO SAUCE

Makes 6 servings

4 cups assorted cut-up
    vegetables (zucchini,
    eggplant, peppers,
    mushrooms)
½ cup GREY POUPON
    Dijon Mustard, divided
1 tablespoon olive oil
1 (7-ounce) jar sundried
    tomato strips in oil,
    drained

1 clove garlic, minced
2 cups light cream or
    half-and-half
1 tablespoon chopped fresh
    basil leaves
1 pound penne pasta,
    cooked
    Grated Parmesan cheese,
    optional

In large bowl, combine vegetables, 2 tablespoons mustard and oil. Place vegetables on broiler pan; broil for 8 to 10 minutes or until golden and tender, stirring occasionally.

In medium saucepan, over medium heat, sauté sundried tomato strips and garlic for 2 minutes. Reduce heat to low and stir in light cream or half-and-half, remaining mustard and basil; heat through.*

In large serving bowl, combine hot cooked pasta, vegetables and cream sauce, tossing to coat well. Serve immediately with Parmesan cheese and garnish if desired.

If sauce thickens upon standing before tossing with pasta, thin with additional light cream or half-and-half.

*Penne Primavera with Sundried
Tomato Sauce*

SWEET & SOUR MUSTARD PORK

Makes 4 servings

1 pound boneless pork, cut into strips

¼ cup GREY POUPON Dijon Mustard, divided

3 teaspoons soy sauce, divided

1 (3-ounce) package chicken-flavored Ramen noodles

1 (8-ounce) can pineapple chunks, drained, reserving juice

½ cup water

2 tablespoons firmly packed light brown sugar

½ teaspoon grated fresh ginger

1 tablespoon cornstarch

2 cups broccoli flowerettes

½ cup chopped red or green cabbage

½ cup chopped red bell pepper

½ cup coarsely chopped onion

2 tablespoons vegetable oil

In medium bowl, combine pork strips, 2 tablespoons mustard and 1 teaspoon soy sauce. Refrigerate for 1 hour.

In small bowl, combine remaining mustard and soy sauce, chicken flavor packet from noodles, reserved pineapple juice, water, brown sugar, ginger and cornstarch; set aside. Cook Ramen noodles according to package directions; drain and set aside.

In large skillet, over medium-high heat, stir-fry vegetables in oil until tender-crisp; remove from skillet. Add pork mixture; stir-fry for 3 to 4 minutes or until done. Return vegetables to skillet with pineapple chunks and cornstarch mixture; heat until mixture thickens and begins to boil. Add cooked noodles, tossing to coat well. Garnish as desired. Serve immediately.

Sweet & Sour Mustard Pork

BISTRO BURGUNDY STEW

Makes 4 servings

1 pound boneless beef
   sirloin, cut into 1½-inch
   pieces
3 tablespoons all-purpose
   flour
6 slices bacon, cut into
   1-inch pieces (about
   ¼ pound)
2 cloves garlic, crushed
3 carrots, peeled and cut
   into 1-inch pieces
   (about 1½ cups)

¾ cup Burgundy or other dry
   red wine
½ cup GREY POUPON
   Dijon Mustard
½ cup beef broth or lower
   sodium beef broth
12 small mushrooms
1½ cups green onions, cut into
   1½-inch pieces
   Tomato rose and parsley,
   for garnish
   Breadsticks, optional

Coat beef with flour, shaking off excess; set aside.

In large skillet, over medium heat, cook bacon just until done; pour off excess fat. Add beef and garlic; cook until browned. Add carrots, wine, mustard and beef broth. Heat to a boil; reduce heat. Cover; simmer for 30 minutes or until carrots are tender, stirring occasionally. Stir in mushrooms and green onions; cook 10 minutes more, stirring occasionally. Garnish with tomato rose and parsley. Serve with breadsticks if desired.

Bistro Burgundy Stew

TOURNEDOS WITH MUSHROOM WINE SAUCE DIJON

Makes 4 servings

¼ cup chopped shallots
2 tablespoons margarine or
   butter
1 cup small mushrooms,
   halved (about 4 ounces)
¼ cup GREY POUPON
   Dijon Mustard, divided
2 tablespoons A.1.® Steak
   Sauce

2 tablespoons Burgundy
   wine
1 tablespoon chopped parsley
4 slices bacon
4 (4-ounce) beef tenderloin
   steaks (tournedos),
   about 1 inch thick
¼ teaspoon coarsely ground
   black pepper

In small saucepan, over medium heat, sauté shallots in margarine or butter until tender. Add mushrooms; sauté 1 minute. Stir in 2 tablespoons mustard, steak sauce, wine and parsley; heat to a boil. Reduce heat and simmer for 5 minutes; keep warm.

Wrap bacon slice around edge of each steak; secure with toothpicks. Coat steaks with remaining mustard; sprinkle with pepper. Grill steaks over medium heat for 10 to 12 minutes or to desired doneness, turning occasionally. Remove toothpicks; serve steaks topped with warm mushroom sauce.

CHICKEN PECAN DIJON

Makes 6 to 8 servings

8 (4-ounce) boneless
   skinless chicken breasts
¼ cup all-purpose flour
¼ cup margarine or butter
2 shallots, chopped
1 clove garlic, minced
⅓ cup sherry cooking wine
1 cup heavy cream*

½ cup seedless grapes, halved
¼ cup GREY POUPON
   COUNTRY DIJON
   Mustard
½ cup Planters® Pecan
   Pieces
   Additional grapes and mint
   leaves, for garnish

Coat chicken with flour, shaking off excess; set aside.

In large nonstick skillet, over medium heat, brown chicken in margarine or butter, in batches, for 5 to 7 minutes or until done. Remove from skillet and keep warm. In same skillet, over medium-high heat, cook shallots and garlic until tender. Add sherry; cook over high heat, stirring to blend in browned bits on bottom of skillet. Reduce heat; stir in cream, grapes and mustard. Cook and stir until sauce thickens. *Do not boil.*

To serve, place chicken breasts on serving platter; top with sauce. Sprinkle with pecan pieces; garnish with additional grapes and mint leaves.

Light cream or half-and-half may be substituted for heavy cream.

CREAMY SEAFOOD PASTA

Makes 5 servings

1 tablespoon margarine or butter
2 tablespoons all-purpose flour
2¼ cups hot milk
⅔ cup GREY POUPON COUNTRY DIJON Mustard
2 tablespoons chopped parsley
1 tablespoon chopped fresh dill weed

1 tablespoon lemon juice
1 pound medium shrimp, cleaned and cooked
1 cup frozen peas
1 pound bow-tie pasta (farfalle), cooked
1 cup cherry tomatoes, halved
⅓ cup grated Parmesan cheese

In large saucepan, over medium heat, melt margarine or butter. Blend in flour; cook 2 to 3 minutes. Gradually whisk in milk; cook and stir until mixture thickens and boils. Reduce heat; simmer for 3 to 4 minutes. Whisk in mustard, parsley, dill and lemon juice; cook 1 minute. Stir in shrimp and peas; heat through.

In large serving bowl, combine hot cooked pasta, shrimp mixture, tomatoes and Parmesan cheese, tossing to coat well. Serve immediately.

HONEY DIJON CORNISH HENS

Makes 4 servings

2 whole Cornish hens, split
  (about 2½ pounds total)
  or 1 (2½-pound)
  chicken, cut up
⅔ cup GREY POUPON
  Dijon Mustard
⅓ cup honey
¼ cup lemon juice
2 tablespoons minced onion
¾ teaspoon minced fresh
  rosemary leaves

½ cup chicken broth or
  lower sodium chicken
  broth
1 teaspoon cornstarch
6 lemon slices, cut into
  halves
  Hot cooked long grain and
  wild rice

Place cornish hens or chicken pieces on rack in roasting pan. Bake at 350°F for 30 minutes.

Meanwhile, in small bowl, blend mustard, honey, lemon juice, onion and rosemary. Use ⅓ cup mustard mixture to brush over hens or chicken. Bake for 30 to 40 minutes more or until done.

In small saucepan, blend remaining mustard mixture, chicken broth and cornstarch. Cook over medium heat until mixture thickens and begins to boil. Add lemon slices; cook for 1 minute. Keep warm.

Serve hens or chicken with rice and heated mustard sauce. Garnish as desired.

Honey Dijon Cornish Hen

COUNTRY KIELBASA KABOBS

Makes 6 servings

½ cup **GREY POUPON COUNTRY DIJON Mustard**
½ cup **apricot preserves**
⅓ cup **minced green onions**
1 pound **kielbasa, cut into 1-inch pieces**
1 large **apple, cored and cut into wedges**

½ cup **frozen pearl onions, thawed**
6 small **red skin potatoes, parboiled and cut into halves**
3 cups **shredded red and green cabbage, steamed**

Soak 6 (10-inch) wooden skewers in water for 30 minutes. In small bowl, blend mustard, preserves and green onions; set aside ¼ cup mixture.

Alternately thread kielbasa, apple, pearl onions and potatoes on skewers. Grill or broil kabobs for 12 to 15 minutes or until done, turning and brushing with remaining mustard mixture. Heat reserved mustard mixture and toss with steamed cabbage. Serve hot with kabobs. Garnish as desired.

DIJON–CRUSTED FISH FILLETS

Makes 4 servings

¼ cup **GREY POUPON Dijon Mustard, divided**
2 tablespoons **margarine or butter, melted**
½ cup **plain dry bread crumbs**
2 tablespoons **grated Parmesan cheese**

2 tablespoons **chopped parsley**
4 (4- to 6-ounce) **firm fish fillets (salmon, cod or catfish)**

In small bowl, blend 2 tablespoons mustard and margarine or butter; stir in bread crumbs, cheese and parsley. Place fish fillets on baking sheet; spread fillets with remaining mustard and top with crumb mixture. Bake at 400°F for 10 to 12 minutes or until fish is golden and flakes easily when tested with fork.

Country Kielbasa Kabobs

SAUTÉED TURKEY MEDALLIONS

Makes 6 servings

2 tablespoons chopped
   shallots
¼ cup margarine or butter,
   divided
2 cups lower sodium
   chicken broth
2 tablespoons reduced
   sodium soy sauce
2 tablespoons balsamic
   vinegar
½ cup GREY POUPON
   Dijon Mustard

¼ cup heavy cream
6 (4-ounce) turkey cutlets
1 medium red onion, sliced
6 sundried tomatoes,* cut
   into thin slices (about
   ⅓ cup)
⅓ cup seedless raisins,
   soaked in 1 tablespoon
   cognac for 1 hour

In medium skillet, over medium heat, sauté shallots in 1 tablespoon margarine or butter until tender. Add chicken broth, soy sauce and vinegar; heat to a boil. Reduce heat; simmer until liquid is reduced by half. Stir in mustard and cream; heat through. Remove from heat; keep warm.

In another skillet, over medium heat, brown turkey on both sides in 2 tablespoons margarine or butter, about 5 to 7 minutes; remove from skillet and keep warm. In same skillet, sauté red onion in remaining margarine or butter until tender. Add tomatoes and drained raisins; cook for 2 minutes more. To serve, top turkey cutlets with onion mixture and warm sauce. Garnish as desired.

If sundried tomatoes are very dry, soften in warm water for 15 minutes. Drain before using.

Sautéed Turkey Medallion

CHICKEN FAJITAS DIJON

Makes 4 servings

¼ cup GREY POUPON
  Dijon Mustard
2 tablespoons vegetable oil,
  divided
2 tablespoons lime juice
1 clove garlic, minced
1 tablespoon chopped
  cilantro
1 teaspoon chili powder
½ teaspoon ground cumin
¼ to ½ teaspoon crushed red
  pepper flakes
1 pound boneless, skinless
  chicken breasts, cut into
  strips

2 small onions, sliced
1 medium red, yellow or
  green bell pepper, cut
  into strips
8 (8-inch) flour tortillas,
  warmed
  Sour cream, chopped
  tomatoes and shredded
  Cheddar cheese,
  optional

In medium bowl, blend mustard, 1 tablespoon oil, lime juice, garlic, cilantro, chili powder, cumin and red pepper flakes. Add chicken, stirring to coat well. Refrigerate for 1 hour.

In large skillet, over medium-high heat, sauté onions and bell pepper strips in remaining oil for 2 to 3 minutes or until tender; remove from skillet. In same skillet, sauté chicken mixture for 5 to 7 minutes or until done. Stir in onion mixture; heat through.

Serve chicken mixture in flour tortillas with sour cream, chopped tomatoes and cheese if desired.

GRILLED BEEF WITH LEMON CAPER SAUCE

Makes 8 servings

⅔ cup GREY POUPON
    Dijon Mustard, divided
⅓ cup olive oil
¼ cup Regina® Red Wine
    Vinegar
1 (2-pound) boneless beef
    sirloin steak
1 cup dairy sour cream*
½ cup minced green onions
¼ cup chopped fresh basil
    leaves

2 tablespoons lemon juice
2 tablespoons chopped
    capers
2 tablespoons chopped
    parsley
Steamed vegetables
    (asparagus, green beans,
    potatoes, red pepper
    strips)

In small bowl, combine ⅓ cup mustard, oil and vinegar. Place steak in glass dish; coat with marinade. Cover; chill at least 1 hour. In medium bowl, blend sour cream, green onions, basil, remaining mustard, lemon juice, capers and parsley. Chill until serving time.

Remove steak from marinade; discard marinade. Grill steak over medium heat for 20 to 25 minutes or to desired doneness, turning occasionally. To serve, slice beef and arrange on serving platter with vegetables. Serve warm with caper sauce.

Lowfat sour cream may be substituted for regular sour cream.

Makes 5 servings

¾ cup GREY POUPON
   Dijon Mustard, divided
1 tablespoon lemon juice
1 tablespoon olive oil
1 clove garlic, minced
½ teaspoon Italian seasoning
1 pound boneless, skinless
   chicken breasts
¼ cup margarine or butter
1 cup chicken broth or lower
   sodium chicken broth

1 cup chopped cooked
   broccoli
⅓ cup coarsely chopped
   roasted red peppers
1 pound tri-color rotelle or
   spiral-shaped pasta,
   cooked
¼ cup grated Parmesan
   cheese

In medium bowl, combine ¼ cup mustard, lemon juice, oil, garlic and Italian seasoning. Add chicken, stirring to coat well. Refrigerate for 1 hour.

Grill or broil chicken over medium heat for 6 minutes on each side or until done. Cool slightly; slice into ½-inch strips and set aside.

In large skillet, over medium heat, melt margarine or butter; blend in remaining mustard and chicken broth. Stir in broccoli and peppers; heat through. In large serving bowl, combine hot cooked pasta, broccoli mixture, chicken and Parmesan cheese, tossing to coat well. Garnish as desired. Serve immediately.

Rotelle with Grilled Chicken Dijon

QUICHE LORRAINE FLORENTINE

Makes 8 servings

1 (10-ounce) package frozen
chopped spinach,
thawed and well drained
1 cup shredded Swiss cheese
(4 ounces)
4 slices bacon, cooked and
crumbled
2 tablespoons chopped green
onions

1 (9-inch) unbaked pastry
shell
3 eggs, slightly beaten
1 cup light cream or
half-and-half
¼ cup GREY POUPON
Dijon Mustard

Combine spinach, cheese, bacon and green onions. Spoon mixture evenly into pastry shell.

In small bowl, blend eggs, cream and mustard. Pour evenly over spinach mixture. Bake at 375°F for 35 to 40 minutes or until knife inserted in center comes out clean. Let stand 10 minutes before serving. To serve, cut into wedges.

DIJON PESTO STEAK

Makes 6 to 8 servings

½ cup finely chopped fresh
basil or parsley
½ cup Planters® Walnuts,
finely chopped
⅓ cup GREY POUPON
Dijon Mustard

1 clove garlic, crushed
1 (2-pound) boneless sirloin
or top round steak

In small bowl, combine basil or parsley, walnuts, mustard and garlic.

Broil steak 5 inches from heat source, about 10 minutes, turning once. Spread top of steak with basil or parsley mixture; broil 2 to 3 minutes more or until lightly browned and beef is cooked to desired doneness. Slice and serve.

Quiche Lorraine Florentine

☗ GREY ☗ POUPON®
1-2-3
QUICK TIPS & MORE

DIPS & SPREADS

RECIPE	1 GREY POUPON MUSTARD	+2 INGREDIENT	+3 INGREDIENT	USE / YIELD
SCALLION DIP	⅓ cup Grey Poupon Dijon Mustard	1 (8-ounce) container sour cream	¼ cup chopped scallions	• Dip • Potato topper Yield: 1 cup
BLUE CHEESE DIP	⅓ cup Grey Poupon Country Dijon Mustard	1 cup prepared blue cheese dressing	2 tablespoons chopped chives	• Dip • Salad dressing Yield: 1⅓ cups
DIJON TARTAR SAUCE	3 tablespoons Grey Poupon Country Dijon Mustard	1 cup prepared tartar sauce		• Fish sandwich spread • Dipping sauce Yield: 1 cup
DIJON LEMON-PEPPER BUTTER	¼ cup Grey Poupon Dijon Mustard	½ cup margarine or butter, melted	1½ teaspoons lemon-pepper seasoning	• Spread on bread • Vegetable or pasta toss Yield: ¾ cup
HONEY MUSTARD DIP	⅓ cup Grey Poupon Country Dijon Mustard	⅓ cup ketchup	1 tablespoon honey	• Dip for chicken • Sandwich spread Yield: ⅔ cup
HICKORY SANDWICH SPREAD	¼ cup Grey Poupon Country Dijon Mustard	¼ cup mayonnaise	¼ teaspoon Wright's® Concentrated Hickory Seasoning	• Sandwich spread Yield: ½ cup

SALAD DRESSINGS, MARINADES & SAUCES

RECIPE	**1** GREY POUPON MUSTARD	**+2** INGREDIENT	**+3** INGREDIENT	USE / YIELD
DIJON VINAIGRETTE	¼ cup Grey Poupon Dijon Mustard	1¼ cups vegetable oil	½ cup red, white or flavored vinegar	• Salad dressing Yield: 2 cups
ORANGE-HONEY MUSTARD DRESSING	⅓ cup Grey Poupon Country Dijon Mustard	⅓ cup honey	⅓ cup orange juice	• Salad dressing Yield: 1 cup
DIJON RED PEPPER DRESSING	¼ cup Grey Poupon Dijon Mustard	1 (7-ounce) jar undrained roasted red peppers, puréed	2 tablespoons honey	• Salad dressing Yield: 1⅓ cups
GINGER DIJON DRESSING	¼ cup Grey Poupon Country Dijon Mustard	1 (8-ounce) container nonfat lemon yogurt	⅛ teaspoon ground ginger	• Salad dressing Yield: 1¼ cups
CAESAR MARINADE	⅓ cup Grey Poupon Dijon Mustard	½ cup prepared Caesar salad dressing	————	• Marinade for pork or chicken Yield: about ¾ cup
DIJON TERIYAKI MARINADE	⅓ cup Grey Poupon Dijon Mustard	2 tablespoons teriyaki sauce	2 tablespoons brown sugar	• Marinade for pork or poultry Yield: ½ cup
ORANGE-GINGER BASTING SAUCE	⅓ cup Grey Poupon Country Dijon Mustard	⅓ cup orange marmalade	1 teaspoon grated fresh ginger	• Basting sauce for ribs, chicken Yield: ⅔ cup
GARLIC PEPPER BASTING SAUCE	⅓ cup Grey Poupon Dijon Mustard	½ teaspoon crushed peppercorn melange	1 clove garlic, crushed	• Basting sauce for steaks, chicken Yield: ⅓ cup
DIJON STEAK SAUCE	⅓ cup Grey Poupon Country Dijon Mustard	1 tablespoon A.1.® Steak Sauce	1 tablespoon brown sugar	• Basting sauce for steaks, pork Yield: about ⅓ cup

QUICK GREY POUPON SAUCES

Cheese Sauce Dijon
• In medium saucepan, over low heat, heat ¼ cup Grey Poupon Dijon Mustard, 8 ounces pasteurized processed Cheddar cheese and ¼ cup milk until cheese melts. Serve over hot cooked vegetables or toss with hot cooked pasta.

Fettuccini Sauce Dijon
• In medium saucepan, over medium heat, heat ¼ cup Grey Poupon Country Dijon Mustard, 1 cup light cream or half-and-half and 2 tablespoons chopped fresh basil until mixture is hot. *(Do not boil.)* Toss with hot cooked fettuccini noodles.

Provençale Sauce Dijon
• In medium saucepan, over medium heat, heat ¼ cup Grey Poupon Dijon Mustard, 1 (14½-ounce) can stewed tomatoes and 2 small onions, quartered, to a boil. Reduce heat to low; cover and simmer 15 minutes. Serve over beef, fish, chicken or rice.

QUICK GREY POUPON TIPS

Try these great tips to add zesty Dijon taste to your foods.

• Stir 3 tablespoons Grey Poupon Country Dijon Mustard into 1 pound prepared deli salad (coleslaw, potato salad, macaroni salad).

• Stir 3 tablespoons Grey Poupon Dijon Mustard and 1 tablespoon brown sugar into 1 (16-ounce) can baked beans.

• For a Dijon omelet or scrambled eggs, whisk 3 tablespoons Grey Poupon Dijon Mustard into 4 eggs before cooking.

• When making grilled cheese sandwiches, spread Grey Poupon Dijon Mustard on sandwiches before grilling.

• Mix Grey Poupon Dijon Mustard into deviled egg filling for extra zip.

• When preparing fish, save calories by brushing it with Grey Poupon Dijon Mustard instead of butter.

INDEX

METRIC CONVERSION CHART

VOLUME MEASUREMENTS (dry)

⅛ teaspoon = 0.5 mL
¼ teaspoon = 1 mL
½ teaspoon = 2 mL
¾ teaspoon = 4 mL
1 teaspoon = 5 mL
1 tablespoon = 15 mL
2 tablespoons = 30 mL
¼ cup = 60 mL
⅓ cup = 75 mL
½ cup = 125 mL
⅔ cup = 150 mL
¼ cup = 175 mL
1 cup = 250 mL
2 cups = 1 pint = 500 mL
3 cups = 750 mL
4 cups = 1 quart = 1 L

VOLUME MEASUREMENTS (fluid)

1 fluid ounce (2 tablespoons) = 30 mL
4 fluid ounces (½ cup) = 125 mL
8 fluid ounces (1 cup) = 250 mL
12 fluid ounces (1½ cups) = 375 mL
16 fluid ounces (2 cups) = 500 mL

WEIGHTS (mass)

½ ounce = 15 g
1 ounce = 30 g
3 ounces = 90 g
4 ounces = 120 g
8 ounces = 225 g
10 ounces = 285 g
12 ounces = 360 g
16 ounces = 1 pound = 450 g

DIMENSIONS

1/16 inch = 2 mm
⅛ inch = 3 mm
¼ inch = 6 mm
½ inch = 1.5 cm
¾ inch = 2 cm
1 inch = 2.5 cm

OVEN TEMPERATURES

250°F = 120°C
275°F = 140°C
300°F = 150°C
325°F = 160°C
350°F = 180°C
375°F = 190°C
400°F = 200°C
425°F = 220°C
450°F = 230°C

BAKING PAN SIZES

Utensil	Size in Inches/ Quarts	Metric Volume	Size in Centimeters
Baking or Cake Pan (square or rectangular)	8×8×2	2 L	20×20×5
	9×9×2	2.5 L	22×22×5
	12×8×2	3 L	30×20×5
	13×9×2	3.5 L	33×23×5
Loaf Pan	8×4×3	1.5 L	20×10×7
	9×5×3	2 L	23×13×7
Round Layer Cake Pan	8×1½	1.2 L	20×4
	9×1½	1.5 L	23×4
Pie Plate	8×1¼	750 mL	20×3
	9×1¼	1 L	23×3
Baking Dish or Casserole	1 quart	1 L	—
	1½ quart	1.5 L	—
	2 quart	2 L	—